NATIONAL GEOGRAPHIC

Ladders

T0308167

NATIVE AMERICANS OF THE PACIFIC NORTHWEST

Read to find out what the Pacific Northwest totem poles represent.

TOWERING TOTEMS

by Debbie Nevins

It's an art. It's a tradition. It's a story. Brightly colored fantastic beasts are carved on a tall cedar tree trunk. There's the killer whale, the raven, the wolf, and the thunderbird. All together, they make a totem pole!

These powerful animals and fierce faces are **symbols** with special meanings. They are not just decorations. They might represent legendary figures or real ancestors. These mighty towers tell stories about the life of a person, family, or tribe.

Totem poles are part of the culture of the Native American people of the Pacific Northwest. These people live on the coast of Oregon, Washington, southern Alaska, and British Columbia. Native Americans probably began making totem poles hundreds of years ago.

Stanley Park in British Columbia, Canada, began collecting totem poles in the 1920s. The newest pole arrived in 2009. Not all of the totems are the real deal. Some are copies of the originals.

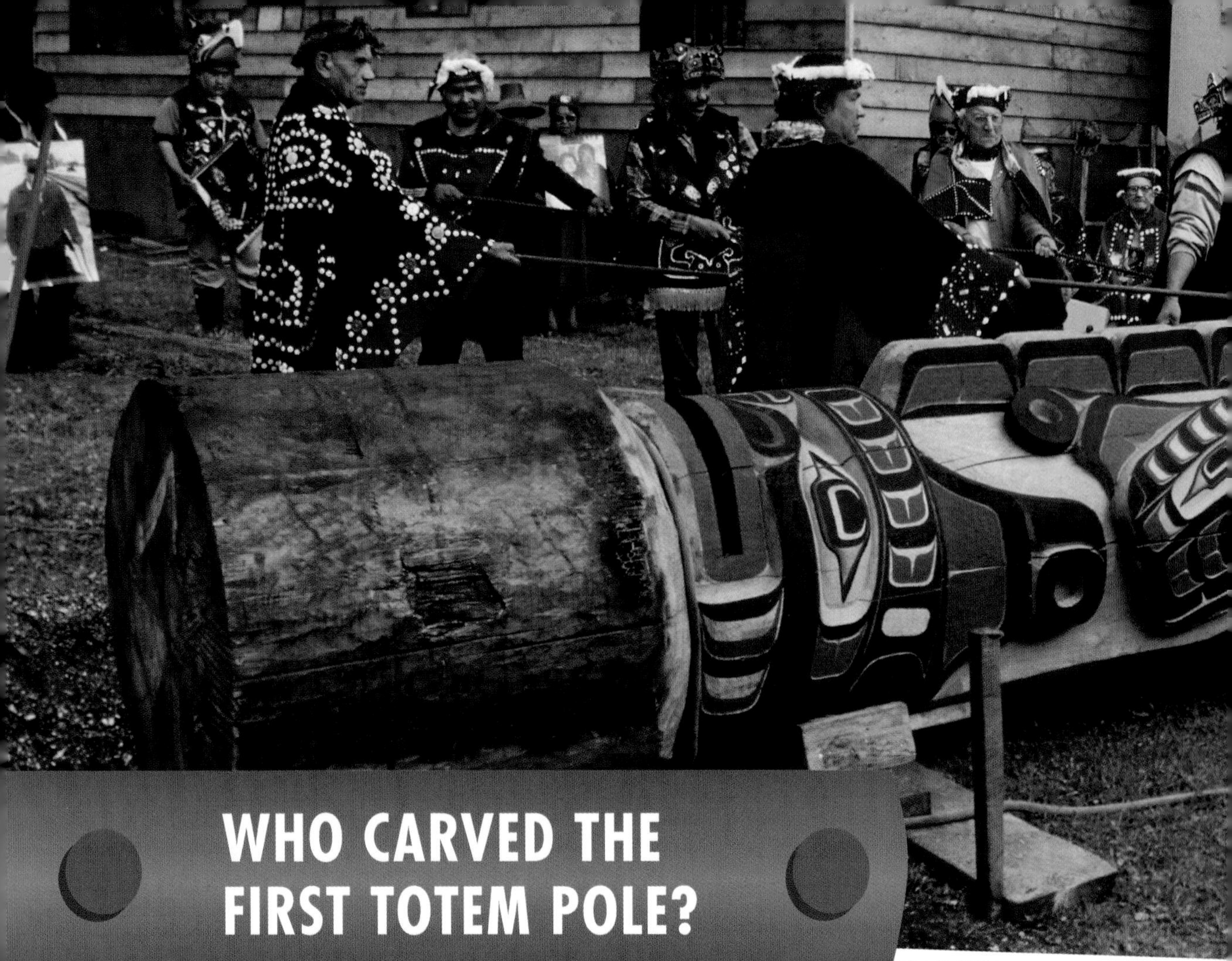

WHO CARVED THE FIRST TOTEM POLE?

This 1860s photograph shows Tlingit people in front of two totem poles, along with photographer Eadweard Muybridge.

The very first totem poles rotted away long ago. But you can learn about them in the myths and legends of the people who first made them.

Years ago, the Pacific Northwest tribes had no written language. So the Haida (HIGH-dah), Tlingit (KLING-kuht), and Tsimshian (CHIHM-she-uhn) tribes told stories to their children instead. These stories told of their history and culture. This is called **oral tradition**. Each generation repeated those stories to their children. They used totem poles to record the stories.

Tribal elders gather in Hee-Ghums, British Columbia, Canada, for a totem pole raising.

Legend says that spirits first taught the people to carve their stories into tall tree trunks. People often used western red cedar. This tree grew in the area. It also had a straight trunk that was easy to carve.

Some totem poles honored the dead. Others celebrated a birth or a wedding. A pole outside the house of an important person showed his or her proud family history. But some poles told stories of crimes. Other poles were carved to embarrass people that did shameful things.

READING A TOTEM POLE

Every face on a totem pole is a symbol. The symbols can mean different things to different tribes. But all of the symbols celebrate the bond between the people and nature. The animals are from the Pacific Northwest: the bear, the whale, the wolf, the eagle, the beaver, the raven. Each represents different qualities. But they mostly represent the land, life, and spirit of the people.

Ellen Neel, the first female Northwest coast carver, made this pole with her uncle.

THUNDERBIRD

The mythological thunderbird is the most powerful spirit to the tribes of the Pacific Northwest. It often tops a totem pole. Legend says that its eyes bring lightning and its wings bring thunder.

BEAR & ORCA

The bear is a symbol of power. It is greatly respected. The orca, or killer whale, stands for family unity. Orcas always stay connected to their families.

MAN & FROG

The frog represents wealth. It is believed to be a force that keeps harmony between people and Earth. Frogs are also believed to be symbols of good luck.

COLORS

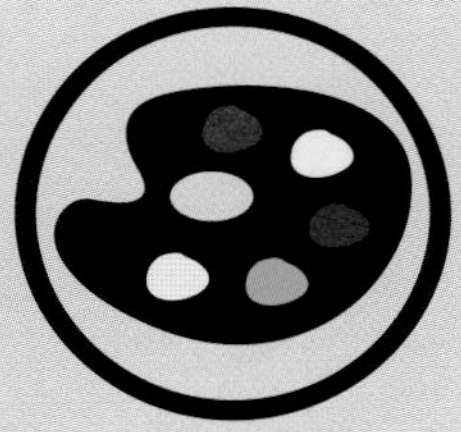

The bright colors on totem poles have meaning, too. Green stands for Earth and nature. White stands for the skies, peace, or death. Blue stands for water and happiness. Red means war, courage, mouths, and tongues. Black means power, and yellow means the sun.

TOTEMS TODAY

The art of totem pole carving was almost lost during the late 1800s. But modern Native Americans are now carving new totem poles. They use traditional methods and hand tools. They are discovering the skill their ancestors used to create those amazing sculptures.

People today can **commission**, or hire, an artist to make a totem pole. An **authentic**, or real, pole must be made by a trained carver from one of the Pacific Northwest tribes. It must be raised in a special ceremony of drumming, singing, and dancing.

Today's Native Americans are proud to learn the art of their ancestors. "When I started carving totem poles, I began to feel connected to my people, my history, my culture," says Tommy Joseph, a Tlingit carver. "My work makes me feel like I'm part of the big picture."

This modern Suquamish carver learned the art from his father.

Check In What do totem poles of the Pacific Northwest represent?

GENRE Folk Tale

Read to find out the orca's origins in the legends of the Pacific Northwest.

The LEGEND of the ORCA

adapted by Laura Mansilla

illustrated by Alexandra Ball

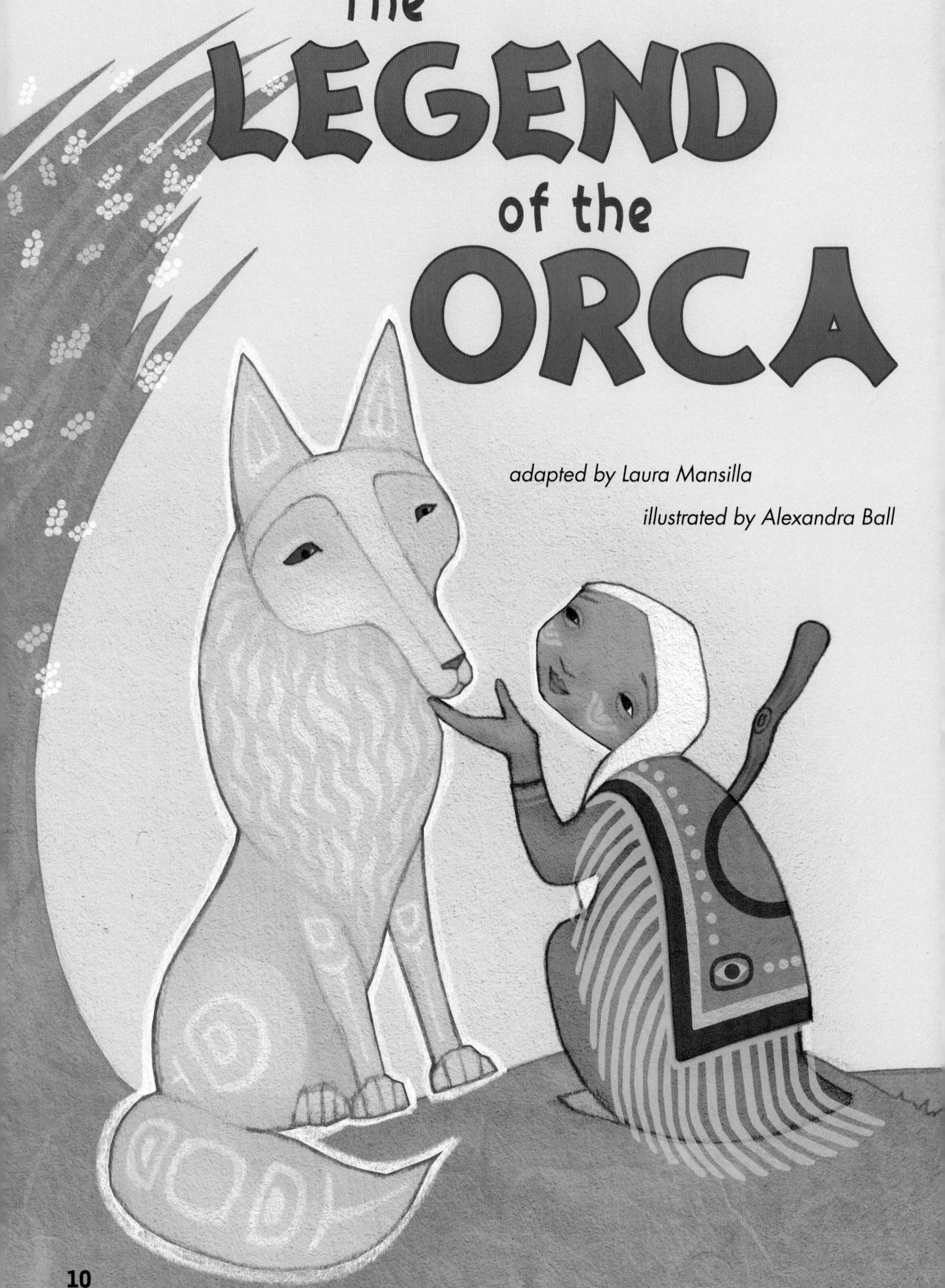

Native Americans have told stories to their children and their grandchildren for generations. These stories help pass on their history, culture, and beliefs. Many Pacific Northwest legends are about sea animals. This traditional Tlingit legend is of the killer whale, also known as the orca.

Long, long ago, Copper Woman created White Wolf. He was her most beautiful creation, so she gave him special powers. White Wolf could run faster, leap higher, and swim farther than the other animals. His fur shone like the stars in the sky. But White Wolf was not like other wolves. It was hard to find friends who could keep up with him. "Grandmother," he asked, "are there no other animals that resemble me?"

Copper Woman was surprised by White Wolf's question. "Why, no, White Wolf. You are truly one of a kind."

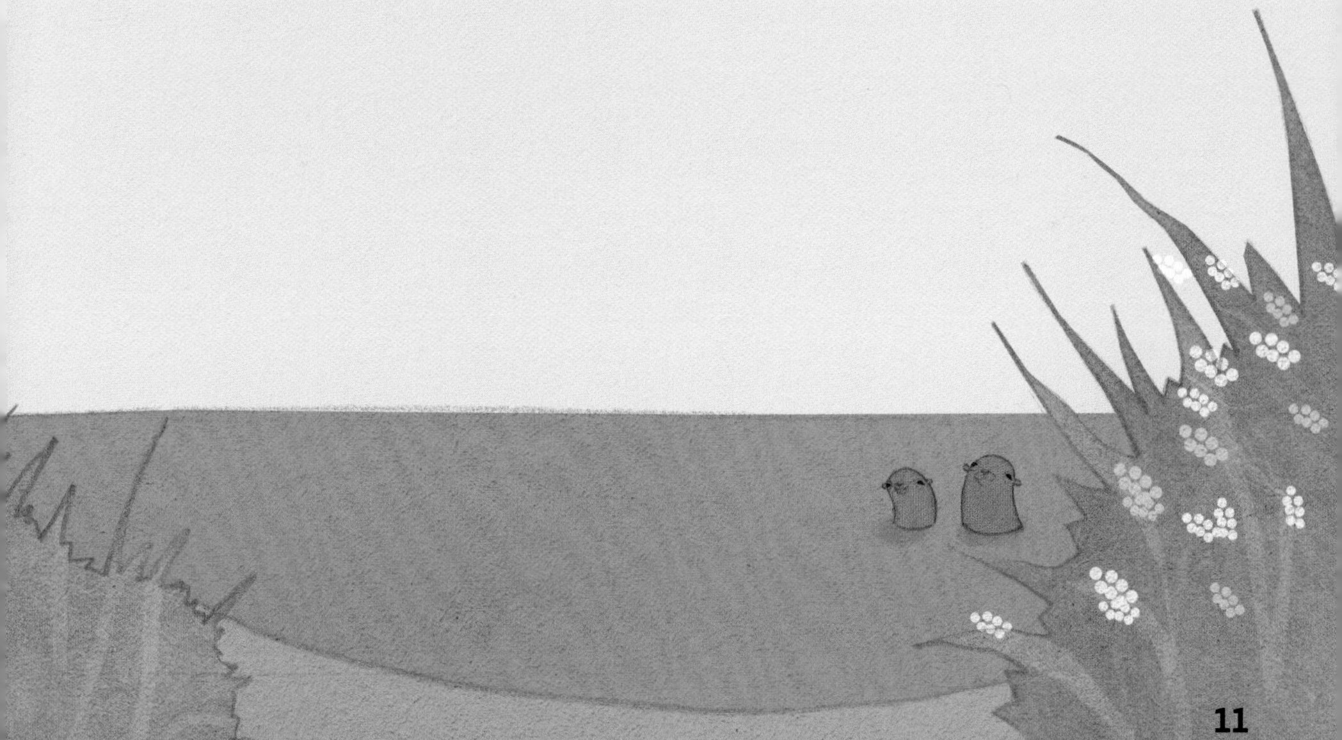

White Wolf was saddened by this. So he searched the world for a pack he could run with. He did not find any other wolves like him. Finally, White Wolf curled up to rest beneath his favorite tree. He fell asleep and had a powerful vision.

"White Wolf," said a mysterious voice. "You must travel to the bottom of the sea. There you will sing about the history of the world!" White Wolf ran to Copper Woman to share his news.

"Oh, my beautiful White Wolf!" sighed Copper Woman. "I see that I must let you go. Be joyful, for you will no longer be alone." Then Copper Woman turned White Wolf into a huge, black killer whale. She painted him with white markings so he would not forget his past as a white wolf. Then Earth's first killer whale, or orca, swam through the sea, singing of the world. Many sea creatures came to hear his beautiful song.

Over time, people began to settle along the coast. Every now and then, they could hear the orca's song. A hunter named Natsilane loved the orca's music. He would listen to its song for hours as he waited for elk to pass by. But Natsilane had three jealous brothers-in-law who wished they had Natsilane's hunting skills. So on a canoeing trip one day, they left Natsilane on an island.

Natsilane feared he would be lost forever. After a long time, a group of sea lions swam up to him. "We will rescue you," the sea lions said, "but we need your help." The sea lions took him to their village and brought him to their sick chief. Natsilane healed the chief using special plants for medicine.

The sea lions cheered. The chief saw that Natsilane was still upset with his brothers-in-law. He said, "Natsilane, you have been wronged. I shall give you the power to carve eight killer whales. Then you must place them into the sea."

Natsilane carved the whales and put them in the water. The carvings turned into real whales. The whales spotted the brothers-in-law on a fishing trip and tipped over their canoe. The brothers were never seen again.

Natsilane respected the mighty orcas. He built a house in a nearby village and named it Orca House. He brought his wife there. The village became their home.

As the village grew, people celebrated the orca. They used its image on arts and crafts. It was very good luck to be splashed by an orca.

Villagers remembered the story of the brothers-in-law. They decided never to harm an orca so that their canoes would not be tipped. Years later, the village chief died. An orca swam near the shore during his funeral. From then on the villagers honored orcas that swam near the shore. They thought the orcas were spirits of humans visiting their family. Today, people watch the orcas swimming by. One of them might be a family member of Natsilane.

Check In How do the villagers feel about the orcas?

GENRE **Biography**

Read to find out how Chief Seattle became a legendary figure in the Pacific Northwest.

CHIEF SEATTLE

by Laura Breedlover

An invading tribe paddled down the White River into Si'ahl's (see-ATH-uhlz) territory. But this young man had a clever plan. When the time was right, Si'ahl's men knocked trees into the water. The trees broke their enemies' canoes and stopped the attack.

Si'ahl's smart planning protected his people. It also made Si'ahl a respected tribal chief at a young age.

Si'ahl was known as "Seattle" to settlers. He was born near the Puget Sound around 1790. In 1792, British explorer George Vancouver arrived with his crew. The tribal people offered them arrows, fish, and carved bracelets. In return they got copper and other metals.

Seattle learned it was important to befriend settlers. But settlers also brought new diseases with them. These diseases killed many of his people.

The sculptor James A. Wehn created the likenesses of Chief Seattle seen here on a 1915 coin (left) and as a statue (right). The statue stands near the Space Needle in Seattle, Washington.

The Puget Sound is a narrow waterway between the city of Seattle and the Olympic Peninsula of Washington. It is Chief Seattle's homeland.

The Warrior from the Puget Sound

Seattle was described as tall and broad, with a booming voice. French traders called him *Le Gros*, or "The Big One."

Chief Seattle was very smart. He was also a brave leader. His main goal was to keep his people safe and in peace. But he could also lead successful attacks when he needed to.

Seattle became known for keeping peace with settlers. They even opened fisheries together in the 1850s. Soon, settlers honored Seattle by naming their village after him.

But the peace between the tribes and the settlers did not last. The U.S. government and the railroad companies wanted the tribal land for a railroad. Seattle and other local chiefs found themselves in a tricky position.

CHIEF SEATTLE'S LIFE

1775

around 1790 Seattle is born in a village near the Puget Sound.

1792 George Vancouver, an early explorer, meets Seattle's people.

around 1826 Seattle is recognized as a leader, or chief.

1833 Fort Nisqually, the first European settlement on the Puget Sound, is founded.

1853 Trading village is named Seattle in Chief Seattle's honor. The Territory of Washington is formed.

1853 Governor Isaac Stevens begins buying up and seizing tribal lands. He removes the tribes to reservations.

1855 Treaty of Point Elliott is signed. It is an agreement that takes away much of the natives' land.

1866 Chief Seattle dies. This sign marks his grave site in Suquamish Memorial Cemetery in Washington.

1875

Chief Seattle's Legacy

The settlers tried to claim the land as their own. This angered the Native Americans who had always lived there.

Isaac Stevens, governor of the Washington Territory, spoke with the tribes in 1855. They created the Treaty of Point Elliott. A **treaty** is a formal agreement between groups to work out a conflict.

The treaty promised that the tribes could stay in the area. But they had to live on lands set aside for them called reservations.

The treaty promised that the tribes could fish where they always had. But the U.S. government did not keep many of the promises it had made in the treaty.

Fighting between the tribes and the government went on for years. The tribes finally signed the treaty. But they lost the land that was their home for more than 10,000 years.

Seattle made a difficult choice by signing the treaty. He knew that the settlers couldn't be stopped. He believed the treaty protected his people by letting them stay in the region.

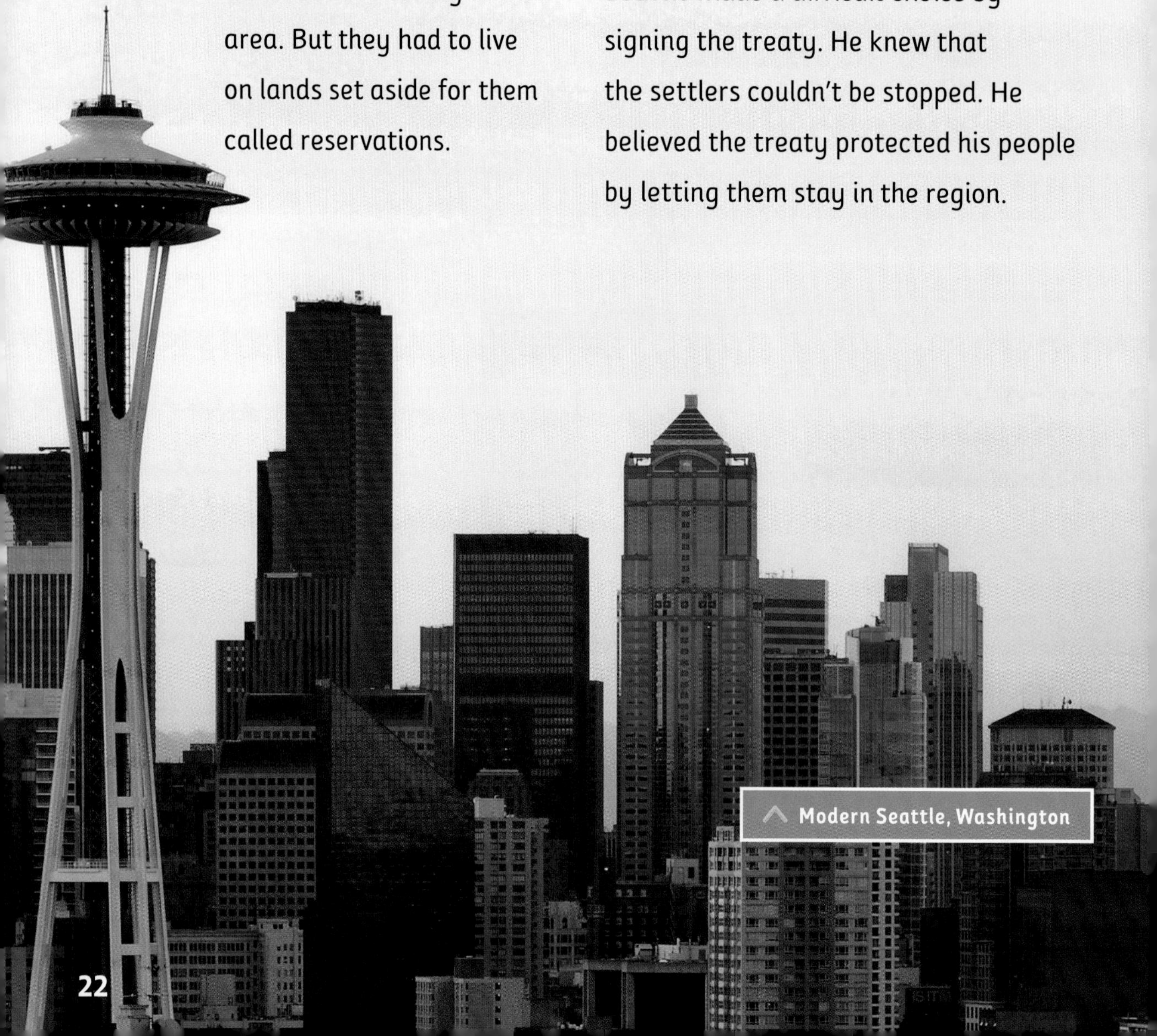

Modern Seattle, Washington

Many tribes were forced to move far away from their homes. Chief Seattle's people still live in the Puget Sound region today. This is his **legacy,** or a valuable gift or act worth remembering from someone in the past.

Chief Seattle spoke about the treaty in a speech. The speech was printed in a Seattle newspaper 22 years later.

Chief Seattle's Speech

There was a time when our people covered the whole land, as the waves of a wind-ruffled sea cover its shell-paved floor. But that time has long since passed away with the greatness of tribes now almost forgotten.

Your proposition seems a just one, and I think my folks will accept it and will retire to the reservation you offer them, and we will dwell apart and in peace.

But should we accept it, I here and now make this the first condition: That we will not be denied the privilege of visiting the graves of our ancestors and friends.

Every part of this country is sacred to my people. Every hillside, every valley, every plain and grove has been hallowed by some fond memory or some sad experience of my tribe.

Check In How do people remember Chief Seattle?

GENRE **Third-Person Narrative** **Read to find out** how Native American culture lives on today.

TLINGIT TRADITION

Nine Tlingit (KLING-kuht) men paddled a hand-carved canoe down the Potomac River to the rhythm of a beating drum. It seemed like an old ceremony. But it was 2008. The canoe was headed to the Smithsonian National Museum of Natural History in Washington, D.C.

Raven Spirit

by Julie Larson

The Tlingit are an **indigenous,** or native, people of the Pacific Northwest. Their homeland is along the coast of southeastern Alaska. Water is an important part of their lives. *Tlingit* means "people of the tides." For centuries, the Tlingit used canoes for transportation. Today, many Tlingit use motorboats.

Doug Chilton is a Tlingit master carver. In 2008, he carved a canoe called the *Raven Spirit.* He used traditional methods, just as his **ancestors** had. He wanted to use this craft to show the importance of the sea in Tlingit history.

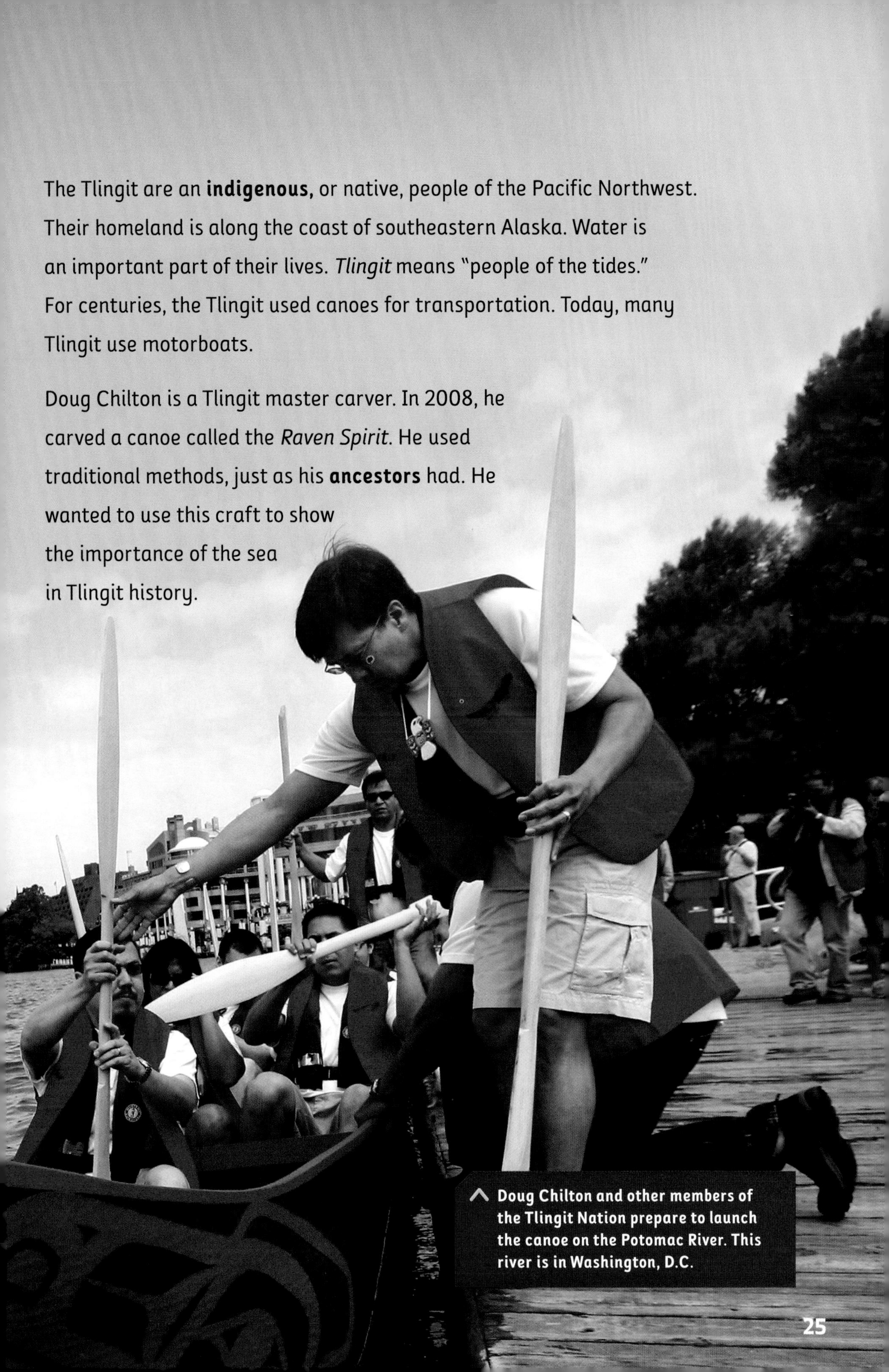

^ Doug Chilton and other members of the Tlingit Nation prepare to launch the canoe on the Potomac River. This river is in Washington, D.C.

CHOOSING A TREE

Chilton gathered a team of artists in Juneau, Alaska. They began to turn a 26-foot-long red cedar log into a beautiful canoe. They used traditional Tlingit tools and methods.

The Tlingit perform ceremonies as the canoe is carved. First, they give thanks to the tree that is chosen for carving. Once Chilton found the tree, he

A drummer marks time for the *Raven Spirit* rowers.

offered food to its spirit. He sprinkled a blanket with goose feathers to protect the tree as it fell. Then he chopped down the tree. Chilton and his team performed the same ceremonies that the Tlingit people performed 500 years ago.

CARVING A CANOE

Modern canoe carvers use chain saws to hollow out a log. This is the only part of the process that is not traditional. Ancient Tlingit carvers would have lit a fire in the center of the log and let it burn. Then they would have hollowed out the burned area with a tool called an *adze*.

Modern carvers then heat water to a near boil. They pour the water into the hollowed log. Steam softens the log. Long, thin pieces of wood called *thwarts* are then placed on the bottom of the canoe. Thwarts give the boat its shape and support. Carvers add designs to the back and sides of the boat.

The canoe is dried and smoked over a fire. Then it is painted. Chilton painted the *Raven Spirit* with a paint made of minerals, salmon eggs, and chewed spruce gum (a gum from trees). The brush was made of bear or porcupine hair!

THE RAVEN

The Tlingit people believe that each canoe has its own spirit. Its carvings often show the canoe's spiritual connection with animals. A carved figurehead of an animal is often on the **prow,** or front of the canoe.

Chilton worked outside to prepare the wood for carving. He saw a raven with an injured wing watching. Then he carved the canoe, and an injured raven was watching again. Could it have been the same bird?

Members of the Tlingit Nation stand with the 26-foot-long red cedar canoe.

Chilton thought it was a blessing that this bird was watching over the project. He added a head of a raven with an injured wing to the prow. He named the canoe the *Raven Spirit*.

The raven often appears in legends of Pacific Northwest peoples. It is thought to be a mix of spirit, human, and bird. The raven can be a trickster. He is also a symbol of change in the world.

Chilton and the team posted videos of their work on the ***Raven Spirit*** on the Internet. The whole world could see the stages of Tlingit carving.

A LONG VOYAGE

The *Raven Spirit* traveled 3,000 miles from Juneau, Alaska, to Washington, D.C. In the capital city, Chilton and several other Tlingit members proudly carried the canoe to the Potomac River. Tlingit drums sounded. Then the group held a ceremony to officially name the canoe.

The *Raven Spirit* is an oceangoing canoe. It is larger than a freshwater canoe and has a different design.

The *Raven Spirit* finally reached the Smithsonian National Museum of Natural History. The canoe hangs from the ceiling, where guests can admire it. The *Raven Spirit* is a symbol of the Tlingit Nation's connection to nature, to the red cedars, and to the sea.

Check In What was the purpose of creating the *Raven Spirit*?

Discuss

1. What connections can you make among the four selections in this book? How are the selections related?

2. Legends often pass on the customs, values, and beliefs of people. What values and ways of life does "The Legend of the Orca" teach?

3. Explain why you think traditional art forms, such as the creation of totem poles and canoes, were important to people of earlier times and are still created and used by people today.

4. How did the settlers' arrival in the Pacific Northwest affect the way of life of the local tribes? How did Chief Seattle express his people's feelings about moving to reservations?

5. What would you still like to find out about the Native Americans of the Pacific Northwest?